LOST WAX

LOST WAX

POEMS BY HEATHER RAMSDELL

UNIVERSITY OF ILLINOIS PRESS

URBANA AND CHICAGO

ACKNOWLEDGMENTS

Grateful acknowledgments to the editors of the following publications in which these poems appeared in earlier form—*Arras:* "Phantom Limb," "First This Then This"; *Big Allis:* "Flag in the Gate," "Ligature"; *Mandorla:* "Nearly Circle," "In Spite of How," "Service of Pointing"; *Sulfur:* "Bridge Segment," "Closet 1"; *Talisman:* "Where Things of a Kind"; *Torque:* "Closet 5"; and *Whatever:* "Surd."

Special thanks to Beverly Watson Matos and Jack Ramsdell, to Ann Lauterbach, and to Marcelle Clements—for their love, instruction, and encouragement.

Library of Congress Cataloging-in-Publication Data
Ramsdell, Heather.
Lost wax : poems / by Heather Ramsdell.
p.   cm. — (The National poetry series)
ISBN 0-252-06706-1 (pbk. : alk. paper)
I. Title. II. Series.
PS3568.A453L67 1998
811'.54—dc21 97-33774
CIP

THE NATIONAL POETRY SERIES

The National Poetry Series was established in 1978 to ensure the publication of five poetry collections annually through participating publishers. Publication is funded by James A. Michener, The Copernicus Society of America, Edward J. Piszek, The Lannan Foundation, and the Tiny Tiger Foundation.

1997 Competition Winners

Sandra Alcosser, *Except by Nature*
Selected by Eamon Grennan, published by Graywolf Press

Martine Bellen, *Tales of Murasaki and Other Poems*
Selected by Rosmarie Waldrop, published by Sun & Moon Press

Robert Gibb, *The Origins of Evening*
Selected by Eavan Boland, published by W. W. Norton

Lisa Lewis, *Silent Treatment*
Selected by Stanley Plumly, published by Penguin Books

Heather Ramsdell, *Lost Wax*
Selected by James Tate, published by the University of Illinois Press

for Garrett Kalleberg

CONTENTS

PROOF BY POINTING

NEARLY CIRCLE

Sad, to shut
to shut other
things into the space left
the space that I left
the space in skewed perspective twisting
foregrounds, sags in glass—*this is your conscience
speaking.* Frontal laughter even
politely refuses the antidote, the closing stroke

later to be fixed, fudged
in memoriam, during the naming of names when you finally show in the
    picture.

And you know who you are. Hold still
just for a moment. Now move. You move
the cloth away from your face. And the face

is vague particles twisting
into thin air, is dust. (Don't I know you?
    I must, I recognize your face in all things and all things must fit
    together, as all stars once did, as all sands did so that sand on the
    floor made sense until we looked closely at it and it spread.)

PHANTOM LIMB

The world kept wandering out on us
returning altered.

Do not look or ask please
fall all the way out

of love with that other
version, trudge.

Forward being only direction.

———

Ice applied to the prisoners' skin gave them second and third degree burns
because blindfolded and told it was hot pokers they hadn't agreed not to
think to be bartered for contiguous amputation.

———

one   one   one

———

A set has ended, again a war has ended again, an argument.

Simultaneous pause in violin, violin, viola

Pablo Casals in afterlife feeling for his hands.

———

In a photo for evidence in an aftermath—
but dust as snow is falling on the mantle
and the body inadvertently breathes, which we see.

Eventually a stem released a petal.

(Did those flowers get looked at or noted, lilies, as they were tossed at some
water? However formed they are the same surrogate what we cannot; their
over-the-counter truthfulness and small expectable deaths level with you,
not caring about carnage as we, who're saying always when something goes
wrong, goes, what went wrong.)

———

As a suicide would from a rail
because she has no bed, is prisoner,

did the form blink—did
she look—or her eyelids protest

as she turned—would she have set
herself also aflame in St. Wenceslaus Square

followed by followers on foot—did
she sleep or affected continue

to face as Lot's wife did the promised
collapse of her city floor under floor

becoming their axis / is the salt.

SURD

A gesturing hand crashes into a microphone, there
at its center, is said to be also the heart
yet this is not an explosion.

Because it resembles nothing else
around what cannot say itself
hang different frames,

strings of high hilarious laughter.

The missing card, an original, has died
in an alley and can't be reached
by Ouija or by wire.

Zeno is laughing his rotten tongue off.

———————

I tolerate what the notebook said but cannot feel my brain.
Tomorrow I'll arise miraculously free of pain.

Otherwise really really fine.

Light alternates with dark then light.
Nutrients travel to fitting departments.
Waste is delivered to its.

Need's other form is something you accept
it comes and slams you over the head.
Nothing enough gets said.

Otherwise really fine.

———

Surrogate connection tries to span
the lacuna, a room of unambiguous design, to assure
this   this   slim
formal hand   a woman's   this
woman's utilitarian hand placed on
the pressure of it on
your available limb
is something, look
at   it   look at it.   I

ran all the way here to tell you this.
This world is manageable.

———

One group of lines means *yes.* Others, strands of hair,
maps of tunnels of the human throat,
tree, a tree, the tree in a brain

near pulses where an energy
means *ow,* sincerely means it.

The circled section where red occurs,
not injury, not roses, not someone articulate
uttering *red* of what else is so

wicked and blunt like a want in a lung.

———

Two lemons in a clean bowl
what liars you are.

What else is here   is   skewed,   a cushion
on a   crappy chair   the green
floor   body   a bowl.   The house

collecting with small said things
is no house but malnutrition
we'll live in but cannot call ours.

The background has sky, estranged
vegetation, a sign. The sky is our only
one against which a violin is tossed
from a window.
               Devastating and beautiful
seem poor examples of true thoughts, use themselves
to exhaustion, moving forward on foot now by night.

Some learn not to take this violence personally.

––––––––

An austere bookshelf fills with complex books, or
a complex bookshelf fills with burlesque books

in which I am a character who wears a bright red dress. In it they say, since
you are good at it and I am not, a gift of pens and pages, like fever deliv-
ered in blankets, write green bright red and brown with its root out, write
it, 2 lemons in a clean white bowl. She says, I'm exhausted by beauty, is
then absconded in interesting light. Black petals sprinkle her white blue
form. Her mirror says it has nothing to say, is shaped like a vortex await-
ing applause.

––––––––

I am a hand on an arm, I thought
metonymic, at least, but am a bag
of parts. Sound falls out of me and in me

and does not break, or broke.
And music says, seductively,
permission—a form of imprisonment.
persimmon—the fruit of the tree dangles, thus

thus, verisimilitude,
and cannot reconcile itself.

These are   not   things
not   images   not   things not
matter.

Tic tic
a pebble in a tin cup, nothing
enough, though no one saw gravity either
carry the avalanche into the valley today.

———

I ran all the way here to tell you this.

A puzzle is of thirty-five squares. One absent by design lets you disrupt
each square, its image and direction toward a comprehensive picture of,
say, a monkey with a blue and red ball or often an alphabet, a leopard
pacing its cage, a scene from Natural America with giant sugar pines fring-
ing the river, which is not essential but that the completed puzzle is a real
puzzle with a missing square.

———

Sometimes the cornice of a building would detach and crush you on the
    street.

Then the river began to melt
which it then completely did refusing
to stand for itself refusing to matter.

ACCIDENTAL

If you've lost control of
it, your foot kicks
out then does break.

Walking, placing a foot
in front to walk
away, difficultly.

Bulging more trapezoidally
out, gap
so people get through.

You can't hurt it it's
hollow.
Nerve beeps.

In the dream of the tube the tube was
solid, froze & stuck
out of the gap.

Tube I know you're in, I saw your eye
moved, a long time
ago, though.

Leaf crushed
to hold the place where
the door shuts.

FIRST THIS THEN THIS

1993 A.D., four seconds later, then fall, intending
to tell itself in these pieces, goes on unaffected. Goes

it was one Thursday, which matters, a marker. I awoke.
I tied the shoe. I ran out. Listing these at you, the story

a circle perpetually finding itself, is ravished, does not end
there. Redundant however useful. Tomorrow, for instance,

I know to wake up. At ten o'clock I would know it is ten,
that I am late, a fissure on a lake of ice, a fissure

water rises through. To let myself know I had not been
moving I moved precluding other

motion. Rain, real rain, obliquely exiting the sky
landed without discrimination meaning

nature tries to do us in, not out of spite.
Apology. A park

punctuated with bright leaves, named
dead leaves, apparently still, filled with other.

A blurry form moving through unresolved form, I entered
the park, or parking lot was it, entered the clearing,

unlike Girl loping through daisies and tall grass
        aimed at unbearable good off-screen
        left, the inimitable flowing skirt
        the hair unnaturalistically aglow—

if the film would roll backward
      steps recoil into their slippers, the drop
      escapes its puddle, she is hurling
      blindly back

forcing the scene to pause a
      fire begins to split the screen, her hand, her hair on
      fire, the field aflame, the sky also burning

would not end there nor would it end. Implied

in every ash a refusal to complete adheres
like fine tissue clings to air threatening
not yet falling off.

The place is the same place, same loss, same necessity.
There, I came upon it, stepped over its body and continued.

HOUSE FACE

Containing little or nothing.
Containing five pages of paper.
And made less human, I.

A chair will be waiting.

A pink door in a black hall
hung, a tongue in her
mouth made less open.

Sounds it sung. Streaks.

Any attempt to run, punished.

To run punished in
falling repeatedly over
a chair a hair a char hail

containing similarity,
almost a figment. I—
I error.

Her in the heart.

MORE ABOUT THE CLOSET

CLOSET 1

I thought I'd say some more about the closet. The closet—my god, the closet is a tangle of sleeves, I could go in but even dreams avoid it. And something is bound to come from that. Some of the shit stacked up in there. Some of the shit stuffed in—I could go on.

I could just go but everything I need I have right here, this [a spoon] and I have this [dress] and here [it's a brick] to show you holding the brick to show you letting go of the brick in a way that is fast, is red or silver, what brick is silver—there is no time now: would you like me to scare you? To show you everything?

For a moment almost forgetting about the closet they emerge from in pilgrim shirts, touching

their own, yanking their
own liver out.

Shirts go in. Shirts come out. Shirts, do not move.

And now I am quite satisfied with myself.

From this box from which I am speaking to you, I am directing you to the left, I am saying, "In." Though I have not been there myself. I must know something like the sensation where you stand.

Are you standing? Are you standing on his softest throat? Are you in his clothing? So he is very close and sees you. Are you liking pulling out his cutting his hair off closing his opening the cavity—are you there, are you standing there?

From which place the whole horizon I see, including descriptive facts and perceptions of the areas most haunting. Including something moving in frequent returns to take on the form of mice rats bald rat tails. Including string rope wire moving at the outer edge of vision, gnawed red packaging bright price tags red rags for windows to wipe the window with to make it clean—

From which place the whole horizon, no footprints leading in, leading out, no center to move out from. From the edge of vision, distances fall equally away, cannot be measured, not reached by foot. By way of reason, to take a stab in the dark—dense, dull as dry clay, hard as common brick, a wall of bricks impenetrable in the common sense, as this is the last part of the house. Beyond; strange music, crowds cheering, crowds breathing, crouching close to the ground to grab a brick to hurl back into the crowd rushing toward a common end

brutally, he said in a reasonable way. It was very clear, what we did to each other was horrible.

I am speaking only for myself. I wasn't there. I've lost some possibility, some range. Each time I opened my mouth it was already public, something had happened to it like blood leaving a wound I am speaking for myself.

Last drops fall from the box I've made a nest and a map from. File: file M. I almost said it. There is no such place. I forget and then remember.

CLOSET 3

                     and can't move. Or
if I move, am quiet, barely shifting side to side within
the closet—days later, the heat off & it being winter
fully inside, not slamming the door, if I had a closet
and I hid in it no one would find me there.

Days, weeks later, already several steps ahead almost
to the kitchen almost turning back—a brief thought
while waiting to sleep—something I wanted to note before
I turn my back on you again:

I was crying. My eye turns red then white again. A recurring theme
in the pattern of relations, neither red or white—I wanted to note
a pain is nowhere, is en route. A recurring theme, slack

as all contingency, angles, branches, mislaid tracks
end here, or sent as emissary represent both
heaven and hell with stylized flames or waves
each neatly its undoing, nor in the between even a line
to have a place: the door.

Wait, there is something I wanted to say before.
I could leave. There.
Doesn't that feel so much better? There.
Doesn't that feel so much better? There

the remainder I'd hoped to be relieved of, going up and down in a slow
elevator, barely up barely down, not quite. There I suddenly move, am
awake and feel a stiffness, arm as it records it.

IN SPITE OF HOW

the floor the wall the wall meet

in spite of how the floor

tilts the individual point

agrees a corner is

fortunate a knob a hand is

incomplete a foot perhaps

no through the door perhaps the individual

has not in the corner incomplete

has not a knob a hand perhaps a corner

opens no a circle is

abstract a circle cannot find its

find its ambition perhaps but thank you

perhaps a hand falls open no

but thank you through the door

in spite of the door

CLOSET 5

for T.B.

Of too many or of few too disparate to cohere
as there are twelve huge piles in this order, one sock in this as
there are many kinds of ants but one platypus.
A ghastly hitch, the absurd, like a gold ring in a pig's ear

for here is enough room to further fill, though not retrieve not arrange
or was it fickleness, doubt
or systems in error, in that
total harmony is fast asleep, in that
transgression outside the system is meaningless. In
partial obliteration a horrible door, where the people live

with the task to see what we have today.
The task to see what we have today
is hard work without without help or way to end because we move in
    and out of this room daily, having cleaned it often something was
    often left over:

excess or repetition, fun outside of use
or endurance following through the gesture,
completion as good in itself, as each instant
in itself, having potential, is.

Go fast for ten minutes, then once completion seems possible,
standing there holding a shirt for a long time.

Let us go at once!
for there is room enough for everything but all. There
is a time, a time merely, and closure belongs
to adjacent planes

to persevere and
blindly, to begin again. To
begin, I mean, by (such quality as ghastly laughter, from the attic)
  vivid/transparent obliteration of the fingerprint, lending
  difficulty the aspect of glass

in which the people live
in tolerable forgetfulness as
no end is *in it*, to the right
a comfortable bed, to the right a room
outside of this room.

WHERE THINGS OF A KIND

In pause, in
decent pause with plausible
care, to push the matter aside

where were we, intentional
streak on glass, we were aware

of our own breathing, meaning
flows from it, uncomfortable

laughter finds a spare
seat in the aisle, the structure,
seen from above, a grid
we cannot stand outside, allows, as

long as the axes hold true, not blow around,
as long as winds don't come, and
we are meant, not error bending, though a bent

hair on a white
tile is also true, because

isn't the idea
to have it
lifelike. Just the other day I

lost my place.
From here on let's leave crumbs, let us
feel free to walk around.

There are fields.
That line looks like a bridge.
A barge a ground, is
that a fire to your left, the trees
stop, bear with us, that
rock is that
hard, there is no need for proof

now, do not
move. Do not anything.

IF IT IS TRUE

FLAG IN THE GATE

for Marcelle

Where a way, a gate to open

On to a gate, agape

Say not anything, something

Human, puff

Of gore flung out to trick the mob

Until we find a door

I think we just walk around

Until a door

Of the puzzle

Of ribbons and squares producing the last surprise

Square, the very base

In sequence, opens

Pitch to blinding, blurring out and snapping in

The long part sailing toward infinity leaving a short stub waving at the root

As if we had managed to escape, now somewhere else

Are having a fabulous time

For the next three minutes

Necessary to continue issue

From each tunnel emptying inward

Groups of voices advance

Necessarily prior

Knowing flattens into one brief curve

In phantom singing swelled to warn them

The characters, the path stop

Where the backdrop curls

As any beginning relies on the later phrase

Coming through the gate, the central column shift.

Do something!

Now!

Before we lose it completely!

I too was once as

Before

And when the lights came on again

There is no distinction, waking in the midst and not in hover in a dream, *there is no idle dream,* if the original is missing, in its drawer something must be found, one thing leading to another, thought bleeding to its next, it is Thursday, it is Sunday. Forgive me for not calling until now, I am going as fast as I can, in going stray ends snagged in the gate, flag unraveling in lax relief

Before we lose it completely, what is it

To lose completely?

To welcome the fateful crumb, press 2

For more

Press 3

For the pliers, the burning splinter of wood

If you'd like to speak with the nurse

Please wait

Darling

You may be wondering why I called you here tonight

Do you like my hat?
Yes, I do.
Do you like my hat?
Yes.
Do you
like my hat? Yes.
Do you like my hat?

SERVICE OF POINTING

     but should we help them   all the
moth's huge
   desire beating   all the helpless
fleet
        bound by design   and
temporally
             fleet   or some procedure
must & should it   staunch the   all   the

convulsive return, as if eros
evolves, such beating from the gentle door would
strike even the young scientist
in the science of that door, that lid. Then
let the past sleep, there will be no dreams for the police

   hide here
           cauldron   pricker bush   shed falling
      and not come back until
                of a big   dark

That's my pile. Things to sort go in my pile. Take nothing, hide nothing
from this pile. I will be home during the weekend. Call me if you need
me for anything. Plans have broken daily, when you speak speak through
a crack as if a door.

                    XO XO   X
                    O incredulous Or

could it be known in the lab what the result would be
enough to leave without looking
with bags with assistance with suicidal resolve

in reflection's stead
the water rocking/rotting clouds
of, clouds of
crowds
of

crows, a field, black, burning
with crows

field of answer

white field
of tracks in the snow the willow
weeps, by design
                —*Family of Willows on White*

pointing strongly
in the fear of pointing, space
in the fear of space, horror
swarms the blink.

PLACED

                  into clear glass jars
      mouths large enough to admit one
             to admit the hand of
          to admit   neither remove
    providing the hand was empty and in a position with fingers
extended
    h nd
          each to its   -in-jar

               successfully removed the lid of the jar
put
           hand into the mouth
                    of the jar
     retrieve

               position to retrieve the

jamming

            position to
   against the mouth
            & tensing would not
the *a*   the *b, c*
    the
             the

    opened spontaneously
    opened in response to verbal stimuli
    opened in response to pain
    did not open

BRIGHT RECEDING

for Roy

With speed the prior body
of the tree could not have foreseen

in orange flakes rising from safety
of, this its release from,
the locus of fire into mossy night,

an imaginary fire in actual night.
Amongst blacknesses, that star already
imploded now is the size of

a rose window, actually
I made that fact up. The sun
came through the window again

by such light, some
burnt trees—such
trees in the yard *make sense*

having incongruities which
occlude both, dread numbs
both—both
include part-answers.
And no research gels.

In being numbers, the shadow faces
turn, locate
one end first, one part, color

of orange and red and black, black
as the black of an eye, please
find me my coat, it says.

It says, you cannot prefer both
the image and itself, you cannot reside
in the possible, henceforth,
resolving to climb inside the solid mound, not see.

MOVEABLE FIGURES

rather deception than retreat, painted in flesh, in the broken arcade,
dust and flecks of red remain

in the instance you and me, by small degrees able aberrations in flesh,
part hiding part enjoying being swallowed

we are very much particles flung here which stuck, are in accordance
with a theory of relations, never in this picture completely enough

from the scientist's window in *Rappaccini's Daughter*, facing a garden of
unnamed flowers, insects in poison, wounds for a mouth in *speaking
from my heart* we are made

today and tomorrow, forever will always be there

your hand or never, look or never, now or how

your hair moved, the stars by small degrees did, let us leave this spot

not exactly putting your finger there, in flesh, first wet then dry, first yes
amid rubble, first involuntary thirst

had shifted, this is not your fault—will I see you again? could we meet
would you like to go, like to the movies, or where you live?

in the instance of yes amid rubble, would you want me always "there"?
would you partway, in a probable future a not undesirable wish

twirling, helpless, insects from the scientist's house, in the theater of
response, I brought you a flower

forever would always be there, what is your complaint—time was very
difficult tonight for tonight we are the real, to wait to stop to say to
kiss to sleep

to have to point to want to go to have, flowers for a flower, this instant

this instant, being foolish, you have broken, this is a bitter ending, I
hate indiscretions, I have to crush you, my heart

half nude, the other half dramatic ruin of the nude, like in true love to
shreds by piece by night unspooling the days events deep threads
catch

here is the plane of the table the meat, and now a finger put in the
abyss

if at all possible, the "I" in "to miss" by small degrees able to conceive
of leaving the theater, eventually offering beloved eventually

IF IT IS TRUE WHAT IS SAID OF THE WORK

we'll never see the result. Refraction
through a medium other than—music
stands subsequent, a sprained surface of actions
of the inner landscape exemplified
by a stick. The stick looks bent. The stick
put through a series of tests, is tossed
striking resemblance, but a ruler must not

keep changing scale, the philosophers needn't be nice.
Later they send an invitation after preventing,
according to logic, attendance. You may never arrive
at a place but cannot remain. Nor is the expedient
replacement flagable. Pack.

They'll carry us out by the collar. The struggle
reluctant to fall wholly to either side.
No reason to mention
neurology, the terms are a stick,
its workings divided with model-makers' skill into
manageable disks, grids placed over the heap.

The table is weighed or the argument table is made of it,
an as-of-yet unbroken version of a crack compared
to an as-of-yet unbroken finger a fist, to a hammer, the table
pinned down with broad duplicity and error, an acute
pinch and incomplete
set of tools to fix the constellation, the moist
eye, the stick, a stick and a stone.

BRIDGE SEGMENT

. 1

No bridge is wanted, we now see,
and bridging is the wrong figure.
 —W. V. Quine

From abutment from
abutment, in a series of angled turns
the path of the circle goes awry.

I keep finding my half on the doorsteps there
where the path, if it is a path, without
formal grip of perspective, too abruptly
arrives. As in the step from a subway.
A plane. In gaudy emergence, want

for a hole through which to go—it's cold
outside—and an eye, an eye and, when it is dark,
any light. Any way to build a way to navigate
to, for the scheme of
the sequence not of footfall not of running fore-
to-aft, a splicing as in a film, in a string's
acquaintedness—of the ones
to the other ones, for a tryst when we are tired.

It is simple and we are tired
and the plan is clear but a clock
ticking throughout, some
aging occurs, an attrition cannot
be stayed. The fine
progression of cracks.
Dumb sleep is lost

in trajectory. In the instance
of moveable parts x misses y
in countless versions of the episode by fractions, plotted
within the blunt dark, by sextant and ship's lamp.

There won't be the closure of books and hands
laid on the table. There was no speeding drum,
not a flag, not a map. It has no legend, and its keys,
I assume, are in the river. There is no bottom.
There is no perimeter, there is nothing if not surface
baldness and its continuous arrangement

which is, exactly, the field.

To call it a prison was mean of them.

Outside, there is no center, between
the dark ground, the dark sky,
at the line difference was no wall
to escape, having already left everything
behind but the task of lunging quickly
toward, where else
is there to go, remember

the stillness of the arc traced
by the falling away of the bodies
which cannot be followed
on foot. They were not just figures.

.2

Then and then a line began but an arrow ensued as drawn without ends

whilst once in the event, before the book fell

during winter, at the same time as morning broke and henceforth

the only apt moment passing in orderly parade a dot

and and delay

the day after that, a delay, at an instant when she was young, the
   instance, suddenly, suddenly, thus

flags of the parted curtain

for the moment, taut with emergency, at a juncture in slow motion,
   formerly these days, often June between the hours of 9 and 2 at ages
   25 through 61, in 1993, a light-year, as they waited the day before
   yesterday when the phone rings, a season ago

ago, when the satellite finally lost its gravity late last week in an
   eventual

of horizon unmodulated by moment

vanishing dot at a subsequent

over end yet-to-land, to an interval, already hours eons later, one calm
   second, an epoch sunset lapsing in perpetuity if, after the last of the
   future in a minute on a Thursday as the day is long, for the past.

.2

Did I say Thursday? I meant June,
how odd.

A tooth
in a glass
of milk,

a missing
tooth.

.3

A book is on a ledge, its message may not be delivered
intact, on time, or arrives wearing knowledge as wig or badge.

The typographer said a missing dot
in the pattern of dots was sad

as when a subject who impersonated the king
was banished beginning the problem of twos

not to suggest an unbroken pattern as paradise

leading to problems of many, none of them
attached, causing impotence, or seamlessly
configured, causing impotence.

Arrival's scrim is painted so.

With a loupe you may see the small elements—points

where communion breaks, the crazing, the leakage,
gaps, where waste is the platform from which to leap—

keep falling through the mesh. Dear Charles,

I'm fine though not myself
I have but three things to say

in all honesty and alarm the book is on a ledge, it speaks
only of losses in margins, I can't
remember the rest. I'm sorry

there's nobody here by that name.

.4

The door, the door's calm
summary slam. I've forgotten,
if I had ever known, the name for it.
There is grace

in the indivisible brick, and gravity.

Agree, the obvious nerve
strands bunched
cloth against the other
nerves is pressure and
a warmth, not love

exactly—a break in the surface, a lip—a lip

had little to do with the problem of the mouth, not the mashing of a mouth
against that mouth because we were glad and bored that day, having al-
ready slept and eaten, plenty of water, sandwiches, milk and figs had
entered the mouth, living bloods of the body within, small breath in and
emitting from the mouth, strings of saliva and, things we found unthink-
able eventually scorched through the mouth, an effusion, a dry wind
through the slender tube opened a flame in the mouth igniting,

you, it said

you, and a pattern emerged,

in the body, she is thinking

of a word. I am thinking of a word, you,
in the last row, nod, if you can hear me.

.5

Snow covers the tracks we left, the dogs
couldn't follow from, past the naked trees,
the slopes had little grip we had to run
quickly and with an expression of certainty
into the field, although

there is no clear route, through this field
the way must be made up
while going along there is a sense
of being

near the river blurred
with ice. The sun

is white. The land,
blind by it, the sky is

snow and horizon
impossible. It is impossible

from this far station in the rows
to tell much

of fault. Of who they are but people
some small distance apart, one

chasing, one running
away, when time,

over the flat ice budged, when

all the sound went out,
still running.

The screen goes black

in the tradition of sleep, one
falls, one would first, night

amongst the animals in act
of matter's stark need for fuel

a twig for heat a morsel
on the bone I love you.

We should have been home by now.

I'm told the life of the fire was brief
though productive. Soon the fog of ashes
will soften and cover this too
in the manner of ash, not to be sorted
then restored. Of course this
is the province, however encrusted
in scaffolds, who can say if the boards
are sound—

           the water is potable, the air improved
but the street has no direction
the street is littered with vacant gloves
figures, the trees
won't bear resemblance
not a leaf, no further need of sirens

           —whether the bridge was
saved if this place is the right the
same or a viable one or was ever
ours to have failed, to be pardoned for.

I am a tourist, amongst the indigenous
tourists, unable to offer directions,
motion in the street is inching
steadily toward or away, a clock
ticking throughout. An exit an arrow
at every turn a clock, some aging occurs.

We noticed the passing facades, stacked
of foils and formica, of stonework
and ash, how they hung from the sky
as a sham for the unseemly wards

and cannot be cheered. This is not
what the book said.

Eventually into the angled streets, we called
wherever we ended up most frequently
our homes, returning the same
half-open eyes and lopped mouth.

.7

You must wear your identification to be
admitted *in the building at all times*
to be seen to belong, without regard
for the referent face, a sense of figure discerned
as by surveillance, the shutter's malfunction
just as the vital face of x upturned.

Who applied to represent themselves?

In an unfair light we are moving
with nauseating speed, either the background
blurs or we blur but the room is a real
room with its attendant rug and door, a series
of arrangement, the random accretions.

A chair has no assignment. We
are also composed.
                    If the clock stopped
the clock wouldn't care. If we're not
the ones we claimed we are—the small
yellowing wouldn't be helped—I am sure
I am real and the others. Our matter
is tolerant, but only prepared
for such blights as have already been imagined.

And the strength of the thread
does not reside in—this isn't the yellow
the fact that some one fibre runs—this
yellow is not realistic, it wants
—through its whole length, but in
the overlapping of many fibres. Memory

coaxed from odd threads of the subsequent found
on a historian's lapel in a sterile bag on a rack of like bags.

Who was last to leave, which one drew
the curtain aside, did the couple,
heard laughing in the room above run, where
was the she last seen, did the hand?
What did the hand?

Who was really last to leave? The lights
stayed on, the films grew clear.

.8

Some agreed to trade their grief for a larger one.

A carrot grows
tiresome, a misery flies
out by moments.

It becomes possible to attend
the banquet wearing char-clothes and be mere,
the one near the door of an ilk in a room of others.

A stain as large as the shirt would go unquestioned.

Sufficiencies, shouts, base laughter arise
with the same uncivilized grace of a fox,
run, laughing away with the bird.
When the profound finally comes
to surface it refers to little trips
to the store for milk with modesty
as of milk, inch-meal, a lightbulb is
exchanged for light meaning the light
at the edge of a table says the same
amount as a face/as the sound of a kicked
shard in the street/as a sentence. The verso
of a violin, having lost its front is sold
for five dollars and fifty cents denoting
a music composed as an instrument to hurl
at passers-by, a song called Please which goes if
if and thus thus, and sings, The Masters sing
there is no act but music, all good, and
free wine for everyone, free laughter
from the floor above, footsteps
of excited preparation, nights, days, elsewhere

the custom is drinks for an hour, fights
for an hour, tears for an hour, elsewhere
only tears, or the custom is tea
without comment, a common laugh
seems at first to delay the memorial
service, then trucks go over steel
palettes in the street, an air conditioner
stops then stops relieving us
of the future, Please do not
force the evidence, we'll respond
to no questions beginning with I, why
all the resuscitation, the long faces
and decline, let go of this. The end

note resonates until the song
gets taken up again, a dirge,

.9

A curtain
left open, the curtain
is open, no

circle discovered in dust-free conditions
or circular mirror in which
to collect the face by piece

that one eventual shard would
drive sense through all the prior

ends, an arc, for a time, that arm
goes casting out toward

as a body in motion tends toward

a certain point, the possible dividing
itself from the case.

As river; the river.

Frankness is in its brown
surface, radiant
waves where the stone went

extend to the far edge of
leaving

clarity's fine dream of
crashing into a wall.

.9A

Heartlessly so the heart
itself is bloodless, a pocket

things are folded in, noumena protrude
as a sock might from a drawer

there a choice to own
the gross bluntnesses of matter, rain

tonight on the precipice,
lamp, you cannot be kind.

LIGATURE

LIGATURE

for Garrett

And the other hand?
Now the other. What are you hiding? Are you
hiding? Fully, closed up, perfectly
in the dark of a cellar
in front of your face a hand
is waving, in the dark are you there are you sure?

The motion is abstract
stone thrown for the sake of seeing
the dark in an hour of—boredom
of the first order, one hell many
chaos, wildly twisting back and forth between

the dark. As no division has been drawn
it is hard to leave.
It is hard to leave this

completely empty
wall.

———

Not that we could.

Picture ice.

Hilarious

how the body slides out

already somewhere
else, ahead already several
steps, already looking back running
toward you and away from you.

There is only one way to read you.
Running toward you and away from you

————

in all directions
stairs—a hell of stairs
between doors, in the choice
of all direction, one way. Extending

all the way
to edge by dull
vibrations in the chest and

opened my mouth and it
was very
very slow

circuit looped together by precise—
the precise point, the focus
breaks, periphery slash the scrim of conscious

thing which

————

comes back to me the moment
I think of something else, memory
breaks into darks. And lights and
all odd grays and subtlety fall out.

To promise at once
comprehension in a flashing
fire is the punishment of the story.

————

Punishment
in the sense of perseverance.

Thank you, by drip
thank you for coming,

cartoons, on top of the steppe
already up here again.

————

Intact though lacking steps along the way, given a system, by necessity
the system breaks, the lever lost, we cannot lift the problem by its edge
step confidently back, to see there is no such thing as low work, as some-
thing sloshing in the house to be mended by material of the house with-
out temptation to wait, as on a Friday night, for a better plan.

————

The figure vacuums
not hearing the phone, the figure vacuums
and nature does not abhor it if
the figure is fire if the fire is
real and mine is the model,

model burning, hand
through the window thrust out.

Once out
the walls of the house
are so small, how ridiculous

laying there. Look at it. It.

————

shoe   shoe
shirt   shirt
book   book   book
garbage
to be burned   gold—gold
teeth in
bins   shoe, the other

shoe, there were three.
In the original ending there were three

conceivable ways to go. Consequence erects itself,
remember the accident? This is a nervous reaction.
What happened happened once.

Now retreat, now parsing. Bridge
and reflection spliced together,
waving no odd fiber or tooth
in extension, monolithically

so simple I ran, so

small small

————

bird plane plume
of smoke rising, same
sky, and the bridge, concrete

wrapped in tape—concrete
which falls from a hand
like a rock from the bridge
through the windshield below

before closure completing the sequence, before
all closure. Completing the sequence
before time fell out, slight falter, a fault or tiny
hole in the argument

———

indicating x.
I know, though what, in this,
is "x"? What numbers, in what
velocity or slant, how
frequent smaller than counting
before counting, how obsessed
through duration's magnificent thrust—

they turn their back, the gods
refuse to answer, sacrilege
though it be to say, because
they do not know.

———

in negligently, carelessly and recklessly failing and
omitting, to have and maintain, in proper condition and in a proper state
failing, so that under proper and, proper, and reasonable control, causing
permitting and allowing, over and along at an excessive rate of speed and
at a greater rate of speed than proper care and

———

caution would permit, fail-
ing thereby to obey and failing to provide and or omitting making proper,

timely use of signals, to be reasonably alert, to look in the direction, to give sign, in negligently, carelessly to come into contact at the intersec

a string
hung from
the pristine, pressed

blue sleeve.
Is empty.

Look, clouds.

ILLINOIS POETRY SERIES
Laurence Lieberman, Editor

NATIONAL POETRY SERIES

Eroding Witness
Nathaniel Mackey (1985)
Selected by Michael S. Harper

Palladium
Alice Fulton (1986)
Selected by Mark Strand

Cities in Motion
Sylvia Moss (1987)
Selected by Derek Walcott

The Hand of God and a Few
Bright Flowers
William Olsen (1988)
Selected by David Wagoner

The Great Bird of Love
Paul Zimmer (1989)
Selected by William Stafford

Stubborn
Roland Flint (1990)
Selected by Dave Smith

The Surface
Laura Mullen (1991)
Selected by C. K. Williams

The Dig
Lynn Emanuel (1992)
Selected by Gerald Stern

My Alexandria
Mark Doty (1993)
Selected by Philip Levine

The High Road to Taos
Martin Edmunds (1994)
Selected by Donald Hall

Theater of Animals
Samn Stockwell (1995)
Selected by Louise Glück

The Broken World
Marcus Cafagña (1996)
Selected by Yusef Komunyakaa

Nine Skies
A. V. Christie (1997)
Selected by Sandra McPherson

Lost Wax
Heather Ramsdell (1998)
Selected by James Tate

OTHER POETRY VOLUMES

Local Men and *Domains*
James Whitehead (1987)

Her Soul beneath the Bone: Women's
Poetry on Breast Cancer
Edited by Leatrice Lifshitz (1988)

Days from a Dream Almanac
Dennis Tedlock (1990)

Working Classics: Poems on
Industrial Life
*Edited by Peter Oresick and Nicholas
Coles* (1990)

Hummers, Knucklers, and Slow
Curves: Contemporary Baseball
Poems
Edited by Don Johnson (1991)

The Double Reckoning of
Christopher Columbus
Barbara Helfgott Hyett (1992)

Selected Poems
Jean Garrigue (1992)

New and Selected Poems, 1962–92
Laurence Lieberman (1993)